PERFECTLY IMPERFECT

WE DON'T HAVE TO BE PERFECT
BECAUSE GOD IS

WRITTEN BY

ANTWALYSE KEA WILLIAMS-HENDERSON

Perfectly Imperfect
"You don't have to be perfect because God is…"

Published by Kingdom Publishing, LLC
1350 Blair Drive Suite F
Odenton, Maryland 21113

Printed in the United States of America

Copyright © 2024 by Antwalyse Henderson

ISBN: 978-1-947741-90-4

All rights reserved. No part of this book may be reproduced or transmitted in any form or by any means, electronic or mechanical, including photocopying, recording or by any information storage and retrieval system without written permission from the author, except for the inclusion of brief quotations in a review.

All scripture quotations are from the King James Version of the Bible. Thomas Nelson Publishers, Nashville: Thomas Nelson, Inc. 1972.

TABLE OF CONTENTS

Foreword 2

Dedication 3

Preface 4

Introduction 5

Chapter 1—In the Beginning 9

Chapter 2—For His Glory 17

Chapter 3—Walking Through It 23

Chapter 4—The Girl on the Refrigerator 27

Chapter 5—Still Facing Giants 31

Chapter 6— The Lord is My Light and Salvation 37

Chapter 7—Waiting for Superman 43

Chapter 8—Parents Be Careful of What Your Children Listen To and Watch 47

Chapter 9—Just Grow a Thicker Skin They Say 51

Chapter 10—School Refusal 53

Chapter 11—Does Anyone Care 59

Chapter 12-- Your Child Angel Beholds the Face of God 63

Chapter 13—Authority of the Believer 67

About the Author 72

FOREWORD

Foreword by Dr. Aaron R. Jones, Pastor of New Hope Church of God

Rev. Henderson has pinned a heartfelt book that I believe should be read by every parent. She articulates crucial moments of parenthood while maintaining her faith and trust in God. Rev. Henderson's transparency and boldness establishes the importance of parental attentiveness needed for their children facing the challenges of life. This book is necessary for today, while we live in times where mental health awareness continues to be on the rise in our nation. More importantly, this book highlights the very critical fact, mental illness has no respect of person and the church needs to be proactive as it relates to mental health.

DEDICATION

This book is dedicated to my daughter, who is the epitome of me, yet stronger, more determined, a lot smarter, more gifted, and anointed for God's work. I love you, daughter!

To my husband Rodney, thank you for being so understanding and supportive. Thank you for reminding me every day that God has a purpose and plan for our lives. Thank you for helping me to see, that it's not that serious and to take time to enjoy life.

To Little Rodney, Mommy "loves" you so much. You are destined for greatness, and you shall be what God has called you to be. To Ben, our bonus kid. Thank you for your "gentle spirit, humility, and steadfastness". Your mom will forever be in our hearts.

To my parents and siblings, there is no way I would have made it through this season without your **"support, love, and humor"**. Our favorite saying, "It's not funny! Oh yes, it is, and we're going to keep laughing until it becomes funny."

To my Pastor and First Lady, Drs. Aaron and Sharon Jones, thank you for tirelessly pouring into us, and pushing us beyond what we could ever fathom or imagine.

To my New Hope Church of God Family, Thank you for your love and support.

PREFACE

She was always a determined little girl who never let a challenge stop her. She was never comfortable with mediocrity and only half succeeding. She always mastered whatever it was she set her mind to do. Consistency was her strong suit. When she wanted to learn how to cartwheel, she didn't stop twirling until she learned. She would come home from school, complete her schoolwork, then play. This explained her high honors throughout elementary and high school. And then…..

Something happened.
        Something changed.
                Something broke.
                          Something was lost.

If you have ever thought about the following:

- "I feel inadequate."
- "I'm not enough."
- "You want me to be perfect, I can't be."
- "The enemy keeps sending negative thoughts."

- "I can't shut off the negative feelings."
- "No one cares"
- "Help Lord, I don't fit in."

This book is for you!

INTRODUCTION

> "For I know the plans I have for you," declares the LORD, "plans to prosper you and not to harm you, plans to give you hope and a future."
> Jeremiah 29:11

When there is a calling on your life or your child's life, the enemy will stop at nothing to stop it and get you to abort the mission. His goal is to get you to self-destruct. He wants to go to the Father and say, "I told you so."

It's happening to God's people each day more and more. If we aren't careful, we will fall into the trap and allow the enemy to win. But occasionally, along will come a soldier for Christ, recognizing the wiles of the devil and telling him where to go and how to get there. They will encourage you to rise up and beat the devil by decreeing and declaring,

> **"No, I told you so! My Father in heaven is greater.
> And I, and my seed were created to win through his Son,
> Christ Jesus!"**

Oftentimes when experiencing a situation, test, or trial, we will begin to believe that it's something we've done. This is not the case all the time. According to **John 9:2-3**, "His disciples asked him, 'Rabbi, who sinned, this man or his parents, that he was born blind?' 'Neither this man nor his parents sinned,'" said Jesus, "but this happened so that the works of God might be displayed in him."

In the Bible, Job was tested. If you're experiencing a difficult time in your life, you may feel like him and start to question the Lord. Not denouncing or cursing God through the hard time, but simply asking "Why?" The word of God tells us in Job 42:1-6 that Job submitted himself to the Lord.

Job's Reply to the Lord:

"I know that You can do all things and that no plan of Yours can be thwarted. You asked, 'Who is this who conceals My counsel without knowledge? 'Surely, I spoke of things I did not understand, things too wonderful for me to know. You said, "Listen now, and I will speak. I will question you, and you shall inform Me. My ears had heard of You, but now my eyes have seen You. Therefore, I retract my words, and I repent in dust and ashes."

Gideon was just like Job, and inquired of the Lord, stating in Judges 6:13,

"Pardon me, my Lord, but if the LORD is with us, why has all this happened to us? Where are all his wonders that our ancestors told us about when they said, 'Did not the LORD bring us up out of Egypt?'

But now the LORD has abandoned us and given us into the hand of Midian."

Gideon wanted to know if God was really with them and if so, then why was all of this happening? Why must we suffer this experience? But God turned to him as the word says in **Judges 6:14**, "Go in the strength you have and save Israel out of Midian's hand. Am I not sending you?"

God was establishing his presence in Gideon's life and establishing him as a mighty warrior. Contrary to what you have been called or referred to in the past, you too are a mighty warrior, and God is with you. However, there will be times in your life in which you will feel inferior and not that of a mighty warrior, no matter who is addressing you.

Whenever we are entering into a season of difficulty, we must know that God has sent us and is with us. It doesn't matter the status of our family, finances, and assets, or who we think we are or are not. God is with us and will fight on our behalf.

JOURNAL PROMPT:

Some tests and trials will be allowed so that God, the Father, may be glorified! Can you trust him through your process? Or will you blame him, preventing his glory from fulfilling its purpose and plan in your life?

Write about a time you had to trust His process and timing.

_____

_____

_____

_____

_____

_____

_____

_____

_____

_____

_____

_____

_____

_____

_____

Chapter 1

In the Beginning

On February 14th, 2006, around 5:00am, I went into labor with our first child. By 8:00am we made it to the hospital, only to be turned around and sent home due to bed unavailability. I had only dilated about 1 centimeter when the doctor sent me home and said to wait until the contractions were five minutes apart. I was experiencing some piercing discomfort and it seemed as if we hit every pothole on the road on the way back.

That entire day I had the most excruciating pain, as if my insides and every bone in my body were twisting and turning. Now I know it's because every part of me was expanding and shifting to deliver our first born, a precious little girl.

The next morning at 8am, I was back at the hospital. A room was available, and the contractions were now 5 minutes apart. At 6pm, I remember crying out from the pain. I was past the point of getting another epidural, and the anesthesiologist told me to just hold on and it wouldn't be long now. I had only dilated a few more centimeters when my doctor came and checked on me. I was furious and had become a bit delirious, with my heart rate and the baby's climbing.

I turned my head to the wall like Hezekiah and began to repent and pray. I made an altar right there in that hospital room by turning my head to the wall, and asked the Lord to forgive me for everything I could think of. I pleaded with him that if he did this for me, I would do whatever for him. The bottom line, I needed HELP, just like the children of Israel in Gideon's day. They were pleading to God out of desperation and not out of love. I was trying to do both or so I thought.

I needed relief, that only God could provide. After my prayer and repenting, my doctor reappeared to check on me, and when she did, she said, "That's weird, you've dilated completely that quickly. Mrs. Henderson it's time to push."

Minutes later, a star was born, and she was perfect. What was even better and miraculous is that the excruciating pain from labor had stopped. Feeling my body return to normal felt so spiritual and supernatural, to think something just like that could change so quickly.

Pregnancy, like most beautiful and uncomfortable events in life, are a state of being. It's temporal doesn't last forever, but what's created from it is worth the pain - so don't rush the process. God is doing something and it's going to be big!

As my daughter was delivered, they let my husband and I hold her. She was something else - so bright eyed, oh my goodness! I couldn't wait to keep her with me, but the nurse returned after a few minutes and said that she needed to be taken for additional testing. They determined she needed to be treated with an antibiotic and had to stay in the NICU, but not to worry because we would all go home in a few days. This was my first battle with **"perfectly, imperfect"**. I thought everything was fine, but my precious newborn daughter needed to be treated for an infection. As I pondered in my heart, "why", I trusted everything would be okay.

I was transferred to another room within the hospital, and went fast to sleep from exhaustion. Each day we spent at the hospital, I would walk down to see her, anxious to take her home but knowing that our discharge day was coming.

The doctor came in the next day and said that my daughter would need to stay a few extra days to make sure she received the proper treatment for the infection, and that she had failed the hearing test and needed to be tested again. This was another round of **"perfectly, imperfect"**. "There's an issue with her hearing?" I thought to myself. My great faith was put to work again. Believing God for the impossible, I was very optimistic. I began to pray and intercede and believed by faith that my baby was fine and would be coming home with me Friday.

Finally, the day came, and her godmother came to see us home. As we were preparing to leave the hospital and waiting for the discharge papers, or so I thought, the doctor walked into the room. In my mind I was getting ready to experience the "new mother glorious wheelchair stroll" through the hallway that I had always dreamed of - the one where you're in the wheelchair holding your newborn and everyone is admiring you as you're being pushed through the hospital. That dream quickly disappeared when the doctor said, "I have good news and bad news. The good news is that your daughter finished the antibiotic and she's fine, but that the bad news is that she failed the hearing test and will have to be retested in two days and must stay here at the hospital."

Devastated, I fell into my husband's arms and wept bitterly. The thought of leaving my newborn in the hospital, let alone my first born, left me hurt, disappointed, and afraid. (What I didn't understand at the time, as life would progress for my daughter there would be many more hard times and tears ahead).

JOURNAL PROMPT:

The Bible says that Mary, the mother of Jesus, pondered things in her heart. The same for Samson's mother. When there is a calling on your child's life, they may endure hardship due to the great anointing and promise upon them. If this is you, don't give up. God will sustain and carry them through even through some of the darkest times.

Can you think of a time when you needed God to see you through?

_____
_____
_____
_____
_____
_____
_____
_____
_____
_____
_____
_____
_____
_____
_____
_____
_____

Chapter 1: In the Beginning

The doctor said, "Mrs. Henderson are you crying? Do you know there are mothers that have to leave their babies in the hospital for months and must come back and forth to visit? You only have two days." In that moment I was being selfish and couldn't think of anyone else. All my life I had thought of others and put them first, but I wanted my baby and for us to all go home as a family.

I was so angry that I made a rash decision and decided not to do the wheelchair ride I had waited my whole life for. I thought to myself, "For what? My baby must stay here at the hospital." Because of this decision I had to sign paperwork basically saying should anything happen to me; the hospital would not be at fault.

As my best friend and godmother of my daughter was trying to console me, she said "I know how you feel, but you may want to re-think walking. The hallways are pretty long."

I was so disappointed and upset, that I didn't listen to her - but, boy, did I regret it! By the time I made it to the car, I was in so much pain all I could do was fall into the car and cry the entire ride home. I had no appetite and there was nothing anyone could do or say. I remember calling the NICU around the clock to check on my baby, getting updates from the nurse on duty, who would say, "oh, I just gave her a bottle," or "I just gave her a bath". The thought of my newborn being cared for by someone else infuriated me, but I knew this was an opportunity to trust God and stand on his Word concerning my family - that he would keep us and never leave or forsake us. This was all a part of the process, for God was working on me and my new journey as a mama.

> **"Thy seed will I establish forever and build up thy throne to all generations." Psalm 89:4**

The day after being discharged was a blur. I remember taking a trip to Walmart just to get out of the house and hiding as I turned down the aisles as I didn't want anyone to see the tears streaming down my face.

My mother was so encouraging and instrumental in this healing process. While she couldn't change the circumstances, she could certainly pray me through, and asked the Lord to give me strength. She knew that as a parent there would be many more days and situations like this in which I would have to trust God "blindly." He had established us, and He was surely with us.

Finally, Sunday arrived. This was the day that I would bring my daughter home. When my eyes opened, I felt so relieved because it was only God that had gotten me through those 48 hours. Mentally and physically, I was exhausted. However, while experiencing those feelings I learned about: **"patience, timing, and imperfection"**.

On the day of my daughter's hearing test, we went to church for 8 am service. At the end of service, we went to the altar for prayer. My Godfather was on duty and he began to pray that all would go well at the hospital. He decreed and declared healing for our daughter. I felt the peace of God rush all over me. I was at peace. Soon after, my husband and I were on our way to the hospital. Once we arrived, we learned she had passed the hearing test and was finally ready to come home. Oh, what joy! We bundled her up and we were off.

Remember the three words: **"patience, timing, and imperfection"**, this is what I learned: **Patience** = the capacity to accept or tolerate delay, trouble, or suffering without getting angry or upset. **(Lord, have mercy, this will make you shout right here!)** God was teaching me how to accept and tolerate a delay. "Delay is not Defeat," and I had to check my attitude. **Timing** = the choice, judgment, or control of when something should be done. God's timing is different than men. He steps into time to deal with us. At his appointed time, things will happen and not a moment before or after. **Imperfection** = the state of being incomplete. A manner or condition of being. **This is temporary and you are not limited to it.**

JOURNAL PROMPT

What have you learned about the lessons of "Patience, Timing, and Imperfection" in your own life?

_____
_____
_____
_____
_____
_____
_____
_____
_____
_____
_____
_____
_____
_____
_____
_____
_____
_____
_____
_____

Chapter 2

For His Glory!

As our daughter grew and progressed as a young child, she had a unique relationship with the Lord early on. It reminded me of myself. I heard the Lord's calling at an early age just as my daughter. In fact, she would speak of visits with Jesus at night. He would visit with her not saying much or give her dreams of him entering the church. She spoke of seeing angels. God's hand was upon her life, and this was just the beginning or so I thought.

One day my daughter asked me if I had listened to the song "Refiner". She began to explain the testimony of the woman singing the song, and how she went through a series of testing. She explained how the woman was tested in the fire of life situations, and came out as pure gold. My daughter stated, "I don't want to sing the song because I don't want the same to happen to me." I thought to myself, why would it happen it to you? Of course, you will have a testimony but not to that extent. How spiritually ignorant of me? What I have now come to learn through our experience is that God is Sovereign! He will cause it to rain on the just and unjust. He's ordered our steps. Whatever God has for you to endure he will walk you through it and stand with you as the fourth person in the fire just like the Hebrew boys. We honestly don't know the extent of the test or trial. And that's fact. However, the anointing will cost you something, but it will be worth it!!!

So, I told her you will be fine it's a worship song. No need to fear. I had no idea that the Lord was preparing my daughter, and our entire family to endure a series of testing that would last over two years. We would be put through fire and refined. And something happened, something changed, something broke. Just like that my daughter began to experience dreams and visions that would shake her very core. In addition, to the spiritual attack she was attacked mentally with severe anxiety that launched her into despair. We were told due to Covid-19, many teens were diagnosed with an anxiety disorder. Her behavior had changed, and some of the things she would say scared anyone listening. It was turmoil.

Oddly enough, in 2013, the Holy Spirit invaded my room at 4am. He began telling me that he wanted me to help bring his daughters out of despair. I was so excited at the time because it was a major call to ministry, and I would soon embark upon leading the Women's ministry. I had no idea the despair call would happen with my own child years later. At the time the Holy Spirit placed the mandate upon my life she was merely a young child. For some reason we have this mentality that it will happen to everyone else except for our family. That's a lie straight from hell. God is no respect of persons remember He is Sovereign!

We become excited about the call of God and direction he's taking us in and those we are to lead. But what happens when the not so glamorous part has to be fulfilled and walked out. When we are literally experiencing all hell breaking loose, are we still excited about the mandate, about the call? This time of testing will literally cost you everything. It's the moment in which you tell the Lord, "I know too much about you to give up. I know too much about you to throw in the towel." You are literally operating out of blind trust. And you can literally hear the Holy Spirit saying, "But my grace is sufficient."

Prior to all of this my daughter loved to worship. While experiencing all of this her worship was different. I felt people would react differently to her dancing in church. At one point, I became embarrassed because I wanted her to do it the "politically correct" Christian way. (Whatever that is.)

> **Doing things the "politically correct" Christian way puts limits on God.**

We must understand that in this moment in time young people are literally fighting for their peace of mind, and it will determine how they worship. Many are worshipping to make it through and to release the burdens, pain, and anguish they are experiencing. Many worship to silence the enemy. The younger generation and anyone, who is grateful to be free, worship is going to look different. We must get ready to receive it, where the **"Spirit of the Lord is, there is Liberty. Jesus came to set the captives free."**

Think for a second and put on the shoes of someone who is constantly being ambushed by the enemy. Thoughts of **despair**. Thoughts of **failure**. Overwhelming feelings of **anxiety**, feelings of **not being good enough** or **imperfect**. Fear of being **ostracized** because of being different. **Not fitting in** on the team. **Not being selected**. **Not being liked** or constantly being **judged**. And to now be in an atmosphere of worship. There are no limits and no boundaries in how they worship. The truth is, saying you must do things the "politically correct" Christian way puts limits on God.

I'm not even free to dance and sing, let alone worship. My daughter found her own way to release **"frustration, trauma from bullying, and passive aggressive people",** to worship the almighty God. One day while at church (after experiencing an anxiety filled weekend I was exhausted from lack of sleep pacing the floor praying and interceding on her behalf), I asked the Lord "why" is this happening and in less than 15 minutes he showed me.

A family christening was being conducted and as we were walking back to our seats, I stepped out into the vestibule. I noticed a mother and daughter sitting out in the hallway. My daughter was following behind me.

After a brief conversation, I quickly gathered the young lady was dealing with some challenges and was unable to attend the main service. Social anxiety prevented her from wanting to attend the youth service. I took a chance with asking my daughter to talk with the young lady, because up until that moment (even though I thought she could relate), my daughter had been nonverbal. To my surprise she immediately began communicating with the young lady. She told her, "I know how you feel, we can sit in youth church for a few minutes and if you feel uncomfortable, I'll bring you to your mom." I was shocked. Not only was my daughter talking and communicating for a few minutes, it was as if she was back to her old self again. They stayed and enjoyed the entire youth service, and the mother was able to attend service and receive the Word she needed.

On the drive home, I told my husband how our daughter was able to encourage another young lady with anxiety to attend youth church and he became overwhelmed with emotion. He was so grateful to God for that glimmer of hope. God was showing us, and the mother of the young lady that it was all for his glory. Remember your situation is a real live testimony and is put on display. Don't despise the circumstance or situation. Embrace it! For you shall reap the harvest if you faint not. Breakthrough is near!!!!

JOURNAL PROMPT:

Have you ever been so overwhelmed with emotion, and your breakthrough soon followed? Write down your experience.

_____
_____
_____
_____
_____
_____
_____
_____
_____
_____
_____
_____
_____
_____
_____
_____
_____
_____

Chapter 3

Walking Through It

There was a point in time when people were wondering what happened to our daughter. They even began to speculate on the relationship between my husband and I, and our home life. Our entire household was under the microscope. We can count the number of people on one hand that came to our home and prayed for our child, or even laid hands and prayed for us.

It was increasingly becoming difficult, and I was lonely. I was now being tested. Having prayed for others and I was now in the need of prayer. Who was going to lift me up before the Lord? Was ministry over for my husband and I? How could we even dare pray for others when things weren't going right for our child? But we didn't give up, because we knew this was a God moment. We continued serving; we continued praying for others; we continued ministering; we continued in the faith. It wasn't ours, it was God's anointing that we were operating in and under.

"And straightway the father of the child cried out, and said with tears, Lord, I believe; help thou, my unbelief." Mark 9:24

Often, we had to pray. The Lord began to allow us to meet those that could relate. Just like that! He began to use people to become transparent and share what they had experienced or currently experiencing and their similar journeys. They were able to share resources and provide much needed support. We needed help!

Through an advocate for the National Association of Mental Illness (NAMI), we received training on how to deal with emotional instability and how to be caregivers. Also, we learned that it's not for us to become defensive or combative, and that it's better to redirect the negative feelings and emotions.

We also learned there is such a thing as being your child's trigger. It was important for us as parents to receive training as well. You certainly aren't to walk in fear, but there are times we can push our children into certain states that aren't healthy. Choose your words wisely!

Life and death are in the power of the tongue. Speak life to your children! **The thief cometh not, but for to steal, and to kill, and to destroy I am come that they might have life, and that they might have it more abundantly (John 10:10).**

JOURNAL PROMPT

Was there a time when you had to speak life to a situation? Please share it below.

_____
_____
_____
_____
_____
_____
_____
_____
_____
_____
_____
_____
_____
_____
_____
_____
_____

Chapter 4

The Girl on the Refrigerator

Due to the anxiety my daughter was placed on home and hospital which consisted of virtual learning. This isn't a good idea due to the paranoia associated with the anxiety disorder. However, at this point we were trying to get her to continue with schooling by any means necessary. During a session of virtual learning, my daughter just wasn't feeling it. As a mom, and her protector and empathetic support system, I was fighting to help her, and it was draining me. This particular day, I felt defeated. I even asked myself, "Why are you here? What good are you? Where is the God in you? Where is the power to overcome?" I had nothing..absolutely nothing.

In that moment, I happened to look up and there on the refrigerator was an old picture of happier days with my daughter. She displayed the brightest smile. I longed to see that smile again. I longed to hear her laugh. I longed for her to speak to me, as we used to do. There is a song by my favorite Christian group, Commissioned. The song is entitled "Do You Still Love Me? It's a conversation the Lord is having with us…and one of the lines mentioned, "I remember the times we used to spend together, the long conversations we used to share with each other, I got to know… Do you still love me like you used to…Do you still love me? I miss my time with you."

In that moment I asked her, "What happened to the girl in the picture? What happened to the smile?"

The grip of anxiety, fueled by the spirit of fear, allowed her inward thoughts (that held her captive), to release her long enough to mutter the lifeless but desperate cry for help… words",

"YOU HAVE NO IDEA WHAT THE GIRL IN THE PICTURE WAS FACING!"

There it was. I was floored, and the feeling of helplessness consumed me once again. I wanted to save her. I wanted to deliver her from this state of being. From birth, my daughter was a fighter. She never gave up and conquered any and everything. I realized that we were both learning this battle wasn't ours, it was the Lord's. I immediately began to pray: **"Father just as you did for Moses, Joshua, and David, fight this battle for us. Send your heavenly host of armies to fight for us. We know that we can't do this without you."** I was reminded in that moment that; **weeping may endure for a night. But Joy cometh in the morning...** I will rejoice!

There are going to be times in your life, as a parent, that when it comes to your child, you will stop at nothing to protect them; and if I must worship my way through to help my child, that is what I was going to do. Because I knew that God was able to do "exceedingly, abundantly, above all I could ask or think according to the power that worketh in me."

Zechariah 4:7, "What are you, O great mountain of obstacles? Before Zerubbabel who will rebuild the temple you will become a plain (insignificant)! And he will bring out the capstone of the new temple with loud shouts of "Grace, grace to it!""

One night as we ventured out to dinner, the (nervous/social anxiety/attack from the pit of hell) "emotional instability" began to torment her. And the scripture came to me was **2 Corinthians 4:17: "For our light affliction, which is but for a moment, worketh for us a far more exceeding and eternal weight of glory."** I spoke just that and said, "God you said this light affliction is but for a moment soon it will be over. Your glory is greater than this moment." We must learn to focus on God's glory during moments like those. Instead of succumbing to the situation began to pray and intercede. Everything must change!

Later that night, the Lord woke me up at 2am with the song, **"Who are you great mountain, that you cannot bow down. Jesus has never lost a battle".** The song was literally playing in my heart. I couldn't believe how loud it was. It was enough to have me sit straight up in the bed.

The Holy Spirit had us to get up and go into her room and intercede. As her Dad anointed her forehead with oil, we stood by her bed and began to pray and intercede, and commanded the mountain to **"dissipate, dissolve, and to go into the sea".**

We entered into spiritual warfare, and intercession, as the Lord led us to do. We remembered that as long as Moses arms were raised, he was winning the battle, but as soon as he let them down, he would lose. We lifted our hands and began to worship because **"this is how we fight our battles".** We began to pray that even when Moses became tired, he had Joshua and Hur to hold his arms up and sit him on a rock. That God would do the same for us, and our child, and that He would send us help, to keep our arms up and sit us on a rock. He sent a very special therapist who works as a "stealth", restoring and helping all of God's children.

JOURNAL PROMPT

Has there been a time in your life where you had to pray your way through? Write about it here.

Chapter 5

Still Facing Giants

It was determined that our daughter would need to be placed on an Individualized Educational Plan (IEP) to accommodate her educational and emotional needs as she dealt with the anxiety disorder, her new diagnosis. The IEP included steps to deescalate situations with elopement, being overwhelmed, social anxiety etc., All of this because she hated school?

One day taking my daughter to school, she got out of the car anxious and hopeful, trying her best to overcome her emotions of fear. We had encouraged and prepared her for the day. She was trying so hard. At that moment she was faced with two students who immediately started laughing at her as she approached the building. She turned around and immediately started walking back to the car.

I began asking, "what happened? All she could muster up was "I hate school" repeatedly. A teacher and I tried to coax her into going into the school, but she wouldn't budge. We managed to walk her up to the door, but she would not cross the threshold. The principal even came out to hold the door for her, but she simply would not budge and planted herself like cement into the sidewalk. I thought to myself, "My God she's strong."

I realized that it was my desire for her to use that same strength and energy to overcome the spirit of fear and conquer it by walking through the door. This experience was just one of our many battles. She would go on to assess situations and if she wanted to enter; "a store, visiting family, the movies, various events etc.," especially if she felt it was too much to handle emotionally and mentally. Often, she would shut down due to social anxiety. There was no reasoning with her.

We found a psychologist to provide additional support and encouragement, and possibly to get her to address the fear of school. Our daughter began to pour out her thoughts about mean people, wondering why they treated her and others that way, when she's done nothing to them. She couldn't seem to shake being overwhelmed and concerned of how others treated her, and it literally had her in bondage.

As a student, my daughter had to complete educational testing, and the facilitators were able to come up with an alternate plan to accommodate her. Even working at home proved difficult, as her thoughts would get the best of her. As for me, I was mentally, physically, and emotionally exhausted. I felt helpless and needed the Lord, desperately.

My prayer during that time was, **"Father, this part of the journey is tough. Even my words are filled with faithless banneker. But I know you desire more for us, Nevertheless, not my will, but let your will be done."** Somewhere along the line our daughter stopped believing that it would be okay. The little girl, who took God at his word, and encouraged all her friends at one point to do it, had lost hope. And now, as her mom, I was experiencing hopelessness too.

When she was younger and in situations where she was scared, I could say, "It's okay you're with us," and get her through the moment. But sadly, as she grew, she no longer believed that. She was believing the lies and the attack of the enemy. The fear began to take over and she began to regress and go into refusal mode. Sometimes I wondered if it was because she could tell I felt like I was losing hope.

One day, I thought maybe getting her out of the house and out to breakfast before there was a big crowd would help. We pulled up to Cracker Barrel like we had done many times before, but this time she refused to go in.

We decided to reroute to Starbucks, but line was too long, and she wanted to go somewhere else. So, we went to another restaurant. We had no luck with that one either, so we ended up going back home.

Chapter 5: Still Facing Giants

I pulled into the driveway, and she got out of the car and went inside the house. I sat in the driveway with tears rolling down my face and prayed for the Lord's help. I didn't want to leave her, but I also didn't want to go back into the house.

Ten minutes later she reappeared at the door, just as I was getting ready to pull out of the driveway. She came onto the front porch and asked, "Mom, can I go with you?" Just like our Father in heaven is overjoyed when we choose him, I felt the same joy. She ran to the car dodging the rain and hopped in. We ended up in the Burger King drive-through. As I sipped on a cup of coffee, I watched her happily nibble on her breakfast sandwich and hash browns. It wasn't the hearty country breakfast I had planned, but it didn't matter because we were together.

In our quest to help our daughter, she went through at least five medications and some over the counter natural supplements but to no avail. Some of the prescribed medications left her rocking and reeling and crying in despair. Others left her like a zombie.

I felt like I had officially failed. I was believing God for a supernatural cure. I was now consenting to medication for the spirit of anxiety? It was supposed to bow, at the name of Jesus. I believed. My husband believed. Why was it taking this long? I was reminded, somethings we must walk through and I had to remember that it wasn't over. Also, it wasn't just about us but our daughter. What was she experiencing? What was she going through? How selfish and unfair of me to put my feelings first. I was quickly reminded that people take medicine for a headache, high blood pressure, diabetes, and numerous other things, and that's considered normal, so why is there a negative connation to take medicines for mental health? Until her "feel good" returned we needed to stay the course. We all have an internal "feel good" meter and if it runs out, you are susceptible to feelings of detriment, lost, and despair. We are far from the peaceful shore.

I learned not to be so defined by the methods used to help your child. But to understand, parents trying to help their children are walking by faith and not by sight. No matter what, our children will not be lost.

JOURNAL PROMPT

Psalm 46:10 says, "Be still and know that I am God." Is there a time you had to be still and trust in the Lord?

_____
_____
_____
_____
_____
_____
_____
_____
_____
_____
_____
_____
_____
_____
_____
_____
_____
_____

Chapter 6

The Lord is My Light and Salvation

"And we know that in all things God works for the good of those who love him, who have been called according to his purpose."
Roman 8:28

To those called God is working. Whatever God has said, it will be accomplished. Think of the Bible, when David was running from Saul - he retreated to the cave of Adullam even though he had just acted like a mad man in front of King Achish. David was human and had a real human moment when he acted out, but he didn't know that God still wanted to use him. He had people who were troubled in the mind, waiting on him to lead them, no matter what was going on in his life.

As believers, God desires to use us for his glory and he has assigned people to us, sometimes right in the middle of our own affliction. No matter what was taking place with our daughter, God still had people for us to lead because of the anointing that's upon our lives. A situation is temporary, but God's purpose and plan is forever.

Many times, I was consumed with what others thought. There came a point in time where people did not want me to lay hands on them or their children, simply for the fact that our daughter was going through something. Often, they thought we may be transferring something. Little did they know, God was healing, setting free, and delivering elsewhere.

But it didn't stop the self-consciousness or worry if service took too long it would consume me. Any place we went, people watched and looked. I would become anxious wondering if the anxiety was going to make her want to leave service or anywhere for that matter. We were literally on a time constraint wherever we went. I began to ask the Lord to cover us, and he did indeed. I stood on, **Psalm 27:1: "The LORD is my light and my salvation; whom shall I fear? the LORD is the strength of my life; of whom shall I be afraid?"** The Lord filled our daughter with the gift of Holy Ghost with the evidence of speaking in tongues. Yes, during all of this! He gave her a supernatural weapon in the midst of adversity. He's Sovereign! He can do anything!

Just because you might be experiencing turbulence, your destiny still must be fulfilled. God is still requiring more of us. Many days from exhaustion I would give in and tell myself that no one cares and would weep endlessly, only to wipe away the tears when someone would enter the room or walk by. Why? Because I had to remain tough. I couldn't let anyone know that I felt as if I was losing the battle.

Sometimes fear would grip my daughter so much that I had to physically pick her up from her bed. There have been times I had to pick her up and place her in the shower and listen to her cry from the fear of possibly drowning in it. I would stand there and intercede on her behalf, praying that God would heal and deliver her from the grips of fear.

On this journey, there was a nurse practitioner we encountered that was extremely helpful and concerned. During a virtual session she began noticing my daughter's slurred speech, they suggested that we take her to the hospital to have a CT scan. It came back normal, but one of the attending physicians at the hospital mentioned that his daughter experienced the same anxiety, and she was having symptoms similar to what our daughter was experiencing. We discovered for most teen girls, the fear, hormonal time leading up to a cycle, Vitamin D deficiency, dehydration, puberty, and more factors were all contributing to a tsunami effect of a downward emotional spiral. We discovered something called Premenstrual Dysphoric Disorder (PMDD). The hormone changes can cause a serotonin deficiency. Serotonin is a substance found naturally in the brain and intestines that narrows blood vessels and can affect

Chapter 6: The Lord is My Light and Salvation

mood and cause physical symptoms such as: "Depressed mood, sadness, hopelessness, or feelings of worthlessness, increased anxiety, tension, or the feeling of being on edge all the time, mood swings. Self-critical thoughts, increased sensitivity to rejection, frequent or sudden tearfulness, increased irritability, anger, or both". If you are underage there isn't a medication than can be prescribed to help cure the disorder. It was one of these factors that brought us to Children's Hospital one Sunday morning, exactly one month after speaking with the physician. My daughter was complaining of feeling weak, so we rushed her to the hospital.

The room was full of sick children, with a long line outside of the door. It was too much; sickness was everywhere, and I ran back to the car to tell my husband we needed to go. He'd pulled off to park the car. Just as I was calling his phone, he was getting off the elevator. He watched my face as I poured out why we needed to leave, and he simply said, "We are here now. Sit outside. I'll wait in line to sign in, and will come and get you when it's our turn."

We found seats outside and while I was enjoying the clean air, I was dreading having to go into the contaminated area. But then I realized there were babies going through it in there, and if I was a minister of the gospel I was to intercede. I began to think, "God, is this the reason you have us here?" I began to intercede quietly for the babies and children that were crying out needing to be touched by the Father. When you are in a situation that you don't understand, cry out to the Father. Ask Him, "Lord, why do you have me here in this place, in this moment? What is it that you desire of me?" Immediately, I went into intercessor mode.

We were assigned to a room inside of emergency that was separated by a curtain. They gave our daughter Tylenol for her pain, and as she laid there on the hospital bed, "WARFARE" ensued. Literally within minutes, a little boy two rooms over let out a blood curdling scream. This went on for a while. He cried and screamed to the top of his lungs. It was so unnerving that I jumped up and started walking the length of the curtain in our area interceding and praying, and I wasn't too quiet about it because of the heightened emotion of the situation. I was praying in my Holy Ghost tongue, interceding as if it was my child. My husband began to call on the name of Jesus, and our daughter, even with her own issues going on, began to pray and war in her spiritual heavenly language right there in the bed. In that hospital triage room, we were fighting in the spirit realm for that little boy.

As we were interceding and on one accord praying on the little boy's behalf, we could hear him begin to calm down and a spirit of peace began to fill the room. The doctor entered their room and we could hear the conversation with his parents and the doctor. The mother explained the boy would always scream and cry hysterically, when encountering doctors. You could literally hear the torment and fear within his cry. It was at that moment; I knew there was a spiritual battle taking place between good and evil concerning the little boy. I believe that day Jesus Christ walked into the room, and won the battle on his behalf. When Jesus Christ enters a situation everything has to change. Things must come under the subjection of the Spirit of the Living God. Believers must understand, the power of God that resides within us. We are literally carrying the next persons deliverance to be set free. Also, obedience is extremely important when it comes to purpose in Christ Jesus.

After the ordeal, we breathed a sigh of relief and our daughter fell fast asleep. Eventually the doctor came in to see us. He asked a flurry of questions and requested testing from head to toe. Seven hours later, each test came back normal. According to science, she just needed fluid for dehydration, but we now understand that our daughter was in that hospital on assignment. Mission Accomplished!

As I look back on the God moments now, I can see how God was truly moving in our lives and how he was with us every step of the way. Trusting God in any situation must be your stance. Without trust, you won't make it. I spoke of blind trust earlier. That's exactly what it will feel like, only because you can't control the situation. You can't see the miracle that will take place. Deliverance is near. We as believers, must stand still and see the salvation of the Lord.

Exodus 14:13, "And Moses said unto the people, "Fear ye not. Stand still, and see the salvation of the Lord, which He will show to you today; for the Egyptians whom ye have seen today, ye shall see them again no more for ever."

JOURNAL PROMPT

Has there been a time in your life where you realized that the Lord was calling you for an assignment? What was the assignment and how did you respond?

_____

_____

_____

_____

_____

_____

_____

_____

_____

_____

_____

_____

_____

_____

_____

_____

_____

_____

_____

_____

Chapter 7

Waiting for Superman

In my quest for my daughter's deliverance (or so I thought), I took her to a small church to receive prayer. Let me preface this encounter with the fact that often we are waiting for someone else to step up and deliver us. We become increasingly upset at others who we thought should be there for us and help us to bear the burden. However, it doesn't always work out like that. **Newsflash:** Jesus has already won the battle. We have the victory. He is our **"Jehovah Nissi - The Lord is my banner".** But as humans we often forget it during seasons of testing, we are to remember the great battles and victories he has already won for us. I was getting ready to learn another important lesson.

My daughter was resistant and upset that I had brought her there. As the people prayed, I began to realize this experience wasn't necessarily for her, but for me. Two of the women began to pray for me, and then told me to pray. As I began to intercede on my own behalf, the women were holding me up. I believe through that intercession that Lord placed a supernatural mantle upon me to strengthen me for the road ahead to endure. **Endurance!** This is required for any time of testing. (And this is also where we fizzle out. We say things like, "I can't take it anymore"; "I have nothing left to give".) However, I walked into that church as a kitten in "despair, helpless, and hopeless", but I left out strong as a lion dripping with HolyGhost fire. You couldn't tell me in the spirit realm, that I was not adorning the most beautiful coat of strength created just for me by the Father's hands. That moment was for me!

My daughter has an amazing voice, which she discovered during an anxiety attack. One night she couldn't sleep and was crying out. We got up ran into her room and began anointing her, the room, and the doorpost.

We began praying and interceding and binding the enemy and the spirit of anxiety. We began to play CeCe Winans album, "Believe For It." She began belting out the most beautiful sound. Her worship began to overtake the room. All my husband and I could do was worship and sit in silence. It was at that moment, we knew there was a gift being birthed in her and the anointing to sing and usher in the presence of God. The atmosphere literally changed.

But I couldn't help but think, where would this gift be used? Because of her struggle, people didn't believe she had such a gift, and nobody wanted to give her a chance to share it. One night my cousin sent me a rendition of the song "Joyful, Joyful" by Pentatonix with singer Jasmine Sullivan. I called my daughter into the room, and she began to belt it out. I asked her what it would cost me, if she allowed me to record her singing. She replied, "a trip to Wawa." One long line and a strawberry smoothie later, I fulfilled my part of the deal and hoped when family saw the video of her gift, they too would be encouraged.

However, when the time came to record her singing, anxiety took over. I started to cry as she walked out of the room, because I knew the enemy had sent this attack against her because he knew of her gift. Truly, my tears fell as I needed help with getting the world to "hear," what I heard, and to "see," what I saw in my daughter. Again, I wanted Superman to come in and help with the situation. Meaning someone else other than me. But the Lord was saying, not so fast there are still some things you need to learn. Honestly, I knew at that moment not to make deals with the spirit that was controlling her. Yes, I said it. Whatever was holding her in bondage wasn't of God. While I knew there were some medical deficiencies, depression, bullying, etc., I knew this was spiritual too and the enemy was manipulating things as well. There are going to be times in which you want to compromise with the situation or circumstance. Stand still and ask the Lord for wisdom on how to handle things at that moment.

Chapter 7: Waiting for Superman

Her dad and I are her biggest cheerleaders, so we got her a voice coach. One day, they were rehearsing "Alabaster Box" by CeCe Winans and it brought me to tears. It's not just the gift, but the anointing that comes through. It's in the oil!

JOURNAL PROMPT

What gifting has God developed in you? When and how was it discovered? What are you doing with that gifting now?

Chapter 8

Parents Be Careful of What Your Children Listen to And Watch

During the pandemic my daughter and son were both on their phones a lot. No matter how much we interrupted with Bible study or had them to take "technology/social media" breaks, it still happened. They were being inundated with everything the internet was offering. Believe it or not too much technology and social media watching can create a portal for "spiritual voyeurism." A voyeur is one who sees, and that can be good or bad, because the enemy lost his privileges as a son of God. His mode of operation has been to overcome the children of God.

The enemy's desire is to take over our human bodies any way that he can, to control us and ultimately destroy us. By accessing our minds, the enemy can infiltrate us with ungodly thoughts, manipulating us to do his will. We must bring balance into what our children and teens are viewing and engaging in these days. Parents we cannot become distracted or disconnected. We must tap in and tune in.

One day my daughter had a dream, and what she told me about it was really disturbing. She never really went into detail of everything, but I knew enough to know that she was dealing with the supernatural and it was a battle between good and evil. The dream was so real that she would hide her phone if she was undressing, because she thought someone was watching her. Once she called me at work to ask if I thought someone was watching her. The fear was really starting to set in, which opened the door for extreme paranoia. I knew it was time to get her some additional help, while continuously praying, anointing her, and believing in God for healing and deliverance.

I contacted a Christian counseling agency. She was assigned a great counselor who really began to get her to open regarding her thoughts and feelings. No doubt she was still being attacked spiritually, but at the same time she was now starting to learn about how to handle those thoughts. Her counselor encouraged her to put her trust in God. My daughter was able to return to school not only because the pandemic had lifted, but mentally. The counselor encouraged her to play sports again and she was great. However, the bullying started because others didn't understand or care that some kids are just different.

Every day as she played her sport and went to practice, she became more and more defensive. If we asked her how practice was, it became an argument. She asked us to pull her out of the sport, but we thought if we did, she would develop a habit of not seeing things through. But we had no idea she was unhappy, it was hard for her to focus, even though she was really good at the sport.

JOURNAL PROMPT

Have you ever been in a situation where you felt like you needed to hide your God-given gift? Explain.

Chapter 9

Just Grow a Thicker Skin, They Say

As parents, especially Christian parents, we teach our children to simply "walk in love." We don't really prepare them to deal with adversity, and as parents, we must let our kids know that if someone mistreats you, don't hang around for it. Yes, exude love and forgiveness, but know when it's time to move on and never internalize the negativity and passive aggressiveness of others, such behavior defines them and not you - it's Christ who defines you, and for that reason, everyone isn't going to treat you as you treat others.

The scripture Matthew 7:12 says, "So in everything, do to others what you would have them do to you." Not everyone enforces this moral principle, and it's sometimes used in a selfish sense, but I feel the meaning behind it is to put yourself in the shoes of others. Would you want to be made to feel poorly or not to be treated well? What if it was you or someone you loved being mistreated?

As parents and humans, sometimes we drop the ball on showing and displaying love because we have been scarred and damaged ourselves, so we no longer enforce it within our homes. The Lord said vengeance is His, yet we find ourselves wanting to take our own revenge and teaching our children "to get them before they get you," which slowly removes innocent trust and forgiveness. Now Love has truly waxed cold, and the younger generations are suffering from it. We must remember that we are to walk in love and be kind.

JOURNAL PROMPT

Have you withheld love and forgiveness because of a situation? Explain the situation/why, and if you have forgiven and extended love?

Chapter 10

School Refusal

"School refusal" is a child or teen avoiding school due to believing something is going to happen there. The basis is a fear of "what if?" A child or teen must feel comfortable and at peace before they do anything, and if there is any type of uneasiness, they will avoid it at all costs. It's up to parents, teachers, educators, therapists, and the child's entire village to talk with them to understand their feelings, and to find out what is causing the anxiety before they reach the flight stage. Flight stage is where the child may feel the need to exit at all costs.

At first our daughter would attend school with no issue, however, over time she began to call me at different times throughout the day. Then it progressed to receiving phones calls during each class, with her leaving out of the class to reach me. It got to the point where she didn't even ask the teacher anymore, she would just walk out and call. The anxiety seemed to increase more and more, and so did my radar for spiritual warfare because I knew the devil was a liar! Within a year's time, our daughter's grades tanked like never before. Her love for school and completing her assignments drastically decreased. We eventually had to pull her out of school and switch to virtual learning, which was not as effective either as she was easily distracted and it was hard for her to pay attention, let alone attend online.

The attacks at night continued. Our daughter would cry out because her thoughts were **"reoccurring" and "attacking her", "stealing her peace" and wanting her to "self-destruct".** Her dad and I would once again grab the oil and go into her bedroom and began to anoint her, the room, and bombard heaven with intercession. We came against the enemy and hell, and she would sleep peacefully after that and into the morning.

We began to take authority over the enemy and would walk the floor decreeing and declaring God's word. We would plead the blood of Jesus over her and began binding the spirit of torment. We knew that our daughter was walking in an amazing calling, but she was faced with opposition from the enemy. (If you notice, I spoke of this a few chapters back. It was a rollercoaster. Up and Down.) Many of you, and your family members may be facing this same kind of torment. Begin to decree and declare that Greater is he that is in you, than he that is in the world! Remember, you have the victory!

When our daughter was younger she wasn't afraid to share Christ with her schoolmates. Often, she was persecuted for believing in Christ, which was just a tactic from the enemy to discourage her until she broke. Kids today are relentless enough, and the dark power of the enemy is used to destroy those in the faith (no matter the age). But we must equip our children with the word of God and encourage them to have a prayer life. **(As you intercede at home invite them into the room to absorb the intercession and presence of God.)**

During this time, the Holy Spirit directed my attention to a book on my shelf by Dr. Rebecca Brown, titled **Prepare for War.** Dr. Brown is also the author of **He Came to Set the Captives Free.** In **Prepare for War,** she stated an important key: We must remember the covenant we have with God the Father when we gave our life to him.

> **"How much more will the blood of Christ, who through the eternal Spirit offered Himself unblemished to God, purify our consciences from works of death, so that we may serve the living God!**
> **Hebrews 9:14**

We reminded our daughter of the covenant that she had with Christ Jesus when he died for us and said that he would never leave nor forsake us. We began to remind her that her **"mind and thoughts,"** could be purified from the works of death and sin and we encouraged her to repent. Why repent? Well, it's simple We can open ourselves to things **"knowingly and unknowingly".** Repenting is washing ourselves clean, ridding anything that's not like Christ Jesus.

I was 12 years old, or maybe even younger, when God began to reveal his power to me, but as He did, so was the enemy. The enemy wanted nothing more than to discourage me from operating in the power of God. What I realized years later as a parent is that God was revealing his power to my daughter, and that we as a family could do more for Him through this situation. It didn't matter what we were faced with, but **the blood of Jesus was more powerful.**

The enemy's biggest lie to my daughter during this time was that she was going to hell and that her salvation wasn't real. We encouraged her to wash her mind in the Blood of Jesus. We printed out these scriptures and posted them on her wall:

Philippians 2:5	"Let this mind be in you that is also in Christ Jesus."
2 Corinthians 2:5	"Casting down imaginations, and every high thing that exalted itself against the knowledge of God and bringing into captivity every thought to the obedience of Christ."
1 John 4:18	"There is no fear in love; but perfect love casteth out fear: because fear hath torment. He that feareth is not made perfect in love."
Isaiah 54:17	"No weapon that is formed against thee shall prosper; and every tongue that shall rise against thee in judgment thou shalt condemn. This is the heritage of the servants of the LORD, and their righteousness is of me, saith the LORD."
Romans 12:2	"And be not conformed to this world: but be ye transformed by the renewing of your mind, that ye may prove what is that good, and acceptable, and perfect, will of God."

At one of her appointments, my daughter's psychologist who walked us through some of the most difficult challenges and dark days she was God sent asked, "who will be working with her to complete assignments, and to make sure she logs onto virtual learning?" The proud and determined me, (one to never back down from a challenge), said "I will." The Psychologist took a deep breath and asked me if I was sure I was up to it. The mind is one of the strongest muscles ever, and that is what the psychologist was trying to convey when she asked if, I was sure. Taking this on was going to be a challenge, and often daunting.

I've had so many breaking points along the way, sometimes having to log off and explain to my daughter's virtual teacher that today just wasn't a good day. Once my daughter told me that she hated school, and everything associated with it. I asked her what was so troubling about it. I can remember from my own experience in school having an occasional bully that had to be prayed away, but overall, I had a good time. Each grade that I went to, I had friends, but in recent years, this has not been the case for many of today's children.

Triggers: My daughter's sixth grade year was a big adjustment, as she went to a private school where I taught. I thought it would be a good thing to have my kids there at the same school every day, and that maybe things might be easier. But by 7th grade, my daughter was shutting down internally, and looking back, I should have understood the warning signs. That's a good point, understanding. Sometimes as parents or guardians we will see something and dismiss it. We must be willing to take the time to further investigate. It could save you both from a lot of turmoil.

She would arrive at the car after school, looking up into the sky, which I now know that she was starting shutdown completely. Oh, how I have beaten myself up for not handling it then, but I thought that I was. I would talk with her and take her out for something she liked, ice cream. In fact, I was trying to overcompensate for the loneliness she felt. The truth was that I should have left her in her previous school and allowed her to continue honing her friendships there (instead of moving her to the school I was teaching).

I felt like I ripped her out of her comfort zone to appease myself and to help me through some new hurdles in life. I began teaching at the school because I lost my previous job, but in taking this position it opened an opportunity to help my son and several others (parents and children). Yep, you got it. My son at that time was dealing with battles of his own, fighting with escapism and flight which started at the age of three. It was at this moment; I begin asking what is upon my children? What calling is upon their lives? What anointing will they walk in? There is a purpose for this. Who will be set free whenever they share their personal testimonies. I am reminded of the scripture in **Isaiah 61:1-3, "The Spirit of the Lord GOD is upon me; because the LORD hath anointed me to preach good tidings unto the meek; he hath sent me to bind up the brokenhearted, to proclaim liberty to the captives, and the opening of the prison to them that are bound."**

There very thing that we are often times running from is what we have been called to do. For through adversity, there is triumph. Close your eyes and think of your last situation. You may have wanted to give up. It may have caused you to question your purpose let alone your existence. However, it's the very thing God has ordained for you to conquer. Take off the running shoes, turn around, and run to it. Know that you aren't by yourself. The Great I AM is with you. This too shall pass! Someone is awaiting your testimony!

JOURNAL PROMPT:

One would ask themselves: What are you running from? Who are you running from? What and who is God calling you to break open the prison doors and set them free with your testimony, and his word?

_____

_____

_____

_____

_____

_____

_____

_____

_____

_____

_____

_____

_____

_____

_____

_____

_____

_____

_____

Chapter 11

Does Anyone Care?

You never know when you will be next. When our children are doing well, we take for granted a breaking point or a turn for the worse because we all have plans for our children, in one way or another. Whether it's the plan God orchestrated for them, or one we couldn't live out. Their ultimate mission is to fulfill their God-ordained plan, and we are to here help them navigate through. I had no idea how driven I was to have my daughter do and be the things that I couldn't be, because she was already carrying it out. Academically she was excelling, and she could cartwheel for goodness sake. I didn't make honor roll until high school and covered it up by simply being the "good kid."

My daughter excelled beyond us at her age. She was on her way to take dual high school and college courses, then it would be off to college. Or so, I thought. That would have been the case in a "perfect" world, but the actual path has been full of learning lessons and God's grace.

I'm reminded of **Isaiah 55:8-9, "For my thoughts are not your thoughts, neither are your ways my ways," declares the LORD. "As the heavens are higher than the earth, so are my ways higher than your ways and my thoughts than your thoughts."** We must re-examine the word perfect. Whatever is imperfect will give the opportunity for God to do the impossible. This is why we are **"perfectly, imperfect"**. Only God can perfect something. While this doesn't give us an out to achieve what we can while on earth, it certainly will cause us to weigh what is most important in life. And that's God's will for our lives.

While virtual learning had been a flop, I completely understood why the psychologist didn't think I should try to facilitate virtual learning on my own with her myself. It was too much. My daughter was now easily distracted, and trying to get her back on track began to wear me thin. Out of total frustration I found myself crying, and air fighting, while secretly and internally screaming "Does anyone care?" If you have children that are learning virtually, I strongly suggest hiring someone to assist your child with completing their assignments if it becomes too much for you. There are aides that can be hired to help assist, and you can work with your local Board of Education to find resources and more information.

But isn't that the lesson in being **"perfectly imperfect?"** Admittedly confessing that I am imperfect, even as a parent. We don't know it all, fall short at times, all while learning and walking through life as well. Parents give yourselves some grace. Just don't give up. We take for granted that our children belong to God and are on loan to us. We are to train them up in the way they should go. That's all we can do in our power. The Holy Spirit will do the rest. Be careful of wanting to control and manipulate, these are tendencies as parents that we can abuse. While guidance is needed, we must be careful. The Holy Spirit is there to guide us through this process.

As I recall dealing with my son, he was around the age of three, when we noticed defiant via determined behavior. He truly needed boundaries, but the way my heart strings were set up, I could not bring myself to set the boundaries nor discipline him. By not doing so caused extreme difficulty for our family and school. There was the occasional, "Don't do that," or "That's not nice." But honestly and truthfully, I should have addressed his behavior and used the word, "No". It would have saved me many a day leaving work early, rushing to the school in time to pull him off the wall because he thought he was Spiderman and he couldn't handle the word, "No". I've got to hand it to the little guy, he was pretty strong and fast. The school and Board of Education meetings that followed were endless. With prayer, structure, and providing our son the support he needed he eventually grew out of that stage.

Think about something. We have thousands of thoughts per day. Our minds are constantly being inundated with thoughts, and we already know by now that we aren't perfect, but we need to remember to be kind to ourselves. Everyone has struggles, but not everyone will be open and honest about them.

In moments of darkness, it may feel as if the walls are closing in on us. Just remember, that God is fighting for us! The forces of darkness are being pushed back by the power of the Holy Ghost and the enemy will be defeated. **"The thing that hath been, it is that which shall be and that which is done is that which shall be done: and there is no new thing under the sun." Ecclesiastes 1:9.** As the scripture states, there is nothing new under the sun. History will repeat itself, however, you must ask yourself am I equipped to handle it? Are you equipped to set boundaries, to help your children. While the walls may be closing in you have the power to overcome. You are not alone and your situation will help someone else.

Oftentimes the enemy will try to isolate us and make us believe that we are the only ones. But someone is waiting on you, and you have what they need to get through this trying time. Remember, it won't always be like this help is here.

JOURNAL PROMPT

**When you are in a dark place, remember these things:
You aren't alone.
You aren't the first.
And you certainly won't be the last.
What would you add to this list?**

Chapter 12

Your Child's Angel Beholds the Face of God

When my daughter was five, she snored terribly. It was something that would wake me up in the middle of the night, and I often found myself sleeping by her bedside to make sure she was breathing correctly. It was a scary time. Her pediatrician referred us to an "Ear, Nose and Throat" specialist and it was determined through tests that she had enlarged adenoids and tonsils. It was recommended that both be removed.

I looked at the doctor and said, "Surgery? She's only 5 years old!" I went into mommy panic mode, but this was different. It was worry, but somehow, I had managed to internalize it more so than showing outwardly. I was pondering over the idea that my young daughter would have to go under the knife, and I found myself having to trust God yet again.

I told my supervisor (at the time) that I would have to be off work for a few days to care for my daughter. He came over to my desk to offer some encouraging words, but as he got up to walk away, he paused and said, "Listen, my son had the same procedure. When they put him to sleep, he began to shake violently. My wife and I were terrified and began crying and screaming. The doctors assured us that everything was okay and that it was just his reaction to the anesthesia, but it was traumatizing none the less so be aware."

I was so grateful that he shared that information because it let me know what to pray against: "any adverse reaction to the anesthesia, and for the Lord to cover our daughter from the beginning until the end." We were trusting God, yet again. On the day of surgery, I was a wreck, but I couldn't show it because I wanted to be strong for her. However, once they got her to sleep (which went off without a hitch, and no complications, praise

God), we were ushered out of the operating room. I sat down in a chair and burst into tears.

It was a trigger for me, unleashing PTSD thoughts from her birth when I had to leave her. The tears flowed, and yet again I had to trust that my Father in Heaven was in control. When the Bible says that our children's angel beholds the face of God, that means that their angel stands before the Lord and receives instructions personally regarding that child. The hand of the Lord is upon our child, and she cannot be plucked out. Ask the Lord to allow you to see your child's angel.

This is my hope for those reading this book - that you'll learn to trust in God. Prayerfully there is something you can take away that will help you in your time of despair and during your personal battle with being "perfectly, imperfect."

Know that God the Father is perfect, therefore we don't have to be, as we embark upon each day in this journey called life. God is truly greater than any situation we may be facing.

JOURNAL PROMPT:

Have you struggled with being perfect? Write down those things you are struggling to achieve, accomplish, and/or experience. Then write down God's promises for your life.

_____

_____

_____

_____

_____

_____

_____

_____

_____

_____

_____

_____

_____

_____

_____

_____

_____

_____

_____

Chapter 13

Authority of the Believer

In 2020, I was the Director over the women's ministry at our church. Our women's retreat was coming up, and I had been seeking the Lord trying to choose the theme. I remember asking Him, "What is it that you want your daughters to know? What do you want to impart into them for this next season?" Prior to planning the retreat, we had a daily 5:00 am prayer call. Each morning I would read and pray **Ephesians 1:15-23:**

"For this reason, ever since I heard about your faith in the Lord Jesus and your love for all the saints, I have not stopped giving thanks for you, remembering you in my prayers, that the God of our Lord Jesus Christ, the glorious Father, may give you a spirit of wisdom and revelation in your knowledge of Him. I ask that the eyes of your heart may be enlightened, so that you may know the hope of His calling, the riches of His glorious inheritance in the saints, and the surpassing greatness of His power to us who believe. These are in accordance with the working of His mighty strength, which He exerted in Christ when He raised Him from the dead and seated Him at His right hand in the heavenly realms, far above all rule and authority, power and dominion, and every name that is named, not only in the present age but also in the one to come. And God put everything under His feet and made Him head over everything for the church, which is His body, the fullness of Him who fills all in all."

Keep in mind this was right before the COVID-19 pandemic impacted the world. Shutting down life as we know it, to stop the spread of the deadly virus, causing a mind-altering, spirit of anxiety and fear that would run rampant upon us all, (especially our children). One morning as I was watching Kenneth Copeland, Billye Brim was on the show, and she was speaking of the **"Authority of the Believer"** in Ephesians 2. She spoke of how she learned this principle when she supported Kenneth Hagin, so I ordered the booklet and began reading it. Immediately, the Lord began to reveal this would be the theme for the women's retreat. The "Authority of the Believer Conference" in 2020 was one of the most powerful conferences! It brought forth unity and a great move of the Holy Spirit amongst God's women. But most importantly, it ignited a supernatural faith in God's women, which blessed and encouraged them through the pandemic. Faith believes that God can, and He will! We have faith that we have been made alive in Christ Jesus and nothing can stop us. We are seated in the heavenlies, and everything is under our feet.

Our daughter completed her eleventh grade year through the grace of God. She's completed 12th grade with a 4.0 and graduated with honors, receiving the President's Education Achievement Award. Yes, God did it in his timing. She is healing each day and showing us that beautiful smile as she continues to trust God. As a family, we are continuing to fight the good fight of faith and walking in the Authority as a Believer.

Upon writing this book, the Lord gave me a dream: Breakthrough is here! Luke 1:45 is being fulfilled in our lives, "And blessed is she that believed: for there shall be a performance of those things which were told her from the Lord". I was in a venue setting up and decorating for some kind of reception. There were little girls on the stage dancing and playing. Some had deformities, and some were disabled. Some people would mistakenly consider them to be **"imperfect."** As I was placing items on the tables the words **"Perfectly, Imperfect"** appeared on the table, and the Lord began to speak to me in the dream. He said, "To the world they are imperfect but to me, they are perfect." Because our Father in heaven is whole, when he completes us, whatever is imperfect (not fully developed, faulty, blemished, or undesirable) is then made whole because of His glory and perfection. We shall be perfected when we are in our glorified bodies, so no need to focus on nor cry over imperfections! For we are "Perfectly, Imperfect!"

We must encourage all whom we encounter with **Revelations 12:11, "And they overcame him, by the Blood of the Lamb and the word of our testimony."** We are overcomers! The enemy is defeated, and there is nothing he can do about it. We win through Christ Jesus and his blood that was shed on the cross at Calvary.

JOURNAL PROMPT:

Now that we are at the end of the book, are you convinced that you no longer must be perfect because Christ is? If so, write down those things that you are willing to surrender to him that have made you feel imperfect.

Help Lord, I need more patience.

I'm wearing thin. I need everything to hurry up and be over.
Not sure how much more I can take. Why me? Will this ever end?
How did we get here?
This isn't fair! What happened? What did I do wrong?
Where did we go wrong?
What did I do to deserve this? How do I get through this?
I'm tapping out. Take this cup from me.
Nevertheless, not my will but let your will be done.
I've learned my lesson. Lord, you know that I know too much about you to give up. I can't throw in the towel, but I want to.
Where is my white flag? I surrender….I need patience Lord!
Help me to understand where she is.
Help to understand what she is experiencing.
Help me to give her the tools to win and overcome…
Help us to walk in "Authority as a believer".

About the Author

Rev. Kea Henderson is the proud wife of Rev. Rodney Henderson Sr. and the mother of two amazing teenagers. She and her husband were blessed to add a bonus son to their family. Rev. Kea holds a Master of Arts degree in Management and Organizational Leadership from APU University and is currently a Program Analyst for Department of Defense. She and her husband are ordained and licensed ministers through Church of God, Cleveland, Tennessee. Rev. Kea attends New Hope Church of God in Waldorf, MD, where Bishop Aaron and Dr. Sharon Jones are her Pastors. Rev. Kea serves as the Director of Effectiveness and Ministry Coordination. She encourages each member to grow spiritually and to serve in their God gifted talents and abilities. She believes in maximizing your potential. Previously, Rev. Kea was the Director of the Women's ministry for seven years, and served nine years on the leadership board. She experienced seeing the women of God become whole, healed from their brokenness, and sharing their testimonies. Rev. Kea stands on Jude 1:24-25, "Now unto him that is able to keep you from falling, and to present you faultless before the presence of his glory with exceeding joy, To the only wise God our Saviour, be glory and majesty, dominion and power, both now and ever. Amen." Her favorite pastime is spending time with her family.

To contact the author for questions, comments or booking, please send correspondence to the following email:

perfectlyimperfectlyproject@gmail.com

www.ingramcontent.com/pod-product-compliance
Lightning Source LLC
Chambersburg PA
CBHW050044080526
44586CB00014B/1443